Autumnblings

Poems & Paintings by Douglas Florian

Greenwillow Books
An Imprint of HarperCollinsPublishers

Library of Congress Cataloging-in-Publication Data

Florian, Douglas.
Autumnblings: poems and paintings / by Douglas Florian.
p. cm.
"Greenwillow Books."
Summary: A collection of poems that portray
the essence of the season between summer and winter.
ISBN 0-06-009278-5 (trade). ISBN 0-06-009279-3 (lib. bdg.)
1. Autumn—Juvenile poetry. 2. Children's poetry, American.
[1. Autumn—Poetry. 2. American poetry.] I. Title.
PS3556.L589 A9 2003 811'.54—dc21 2002029780

1 2 3 4 5 6 7 8 9 10
First Edition

Contents

AUTUMNBLINGS

Autumn f
        a
          l
            l
                s in late September.
A time to savor and remember:
Where did all the green things go,
As autumn *tumbled* into snow?

WHAT I LOVE ABOUT AUTUMN

Apple picking
Frisbee flicking
Falling leaves
Bracing breeze
Flying kites
Cool crisp nights
Trick or treat
(Sweets to eat)
Pumpkin pies
Clear blue skies
Fireplaces
Relay races
Football games—
I love that autumn has two names.

What i hate about autumn

Summer's done
Not much sun
Back to school
Air's too cool
Winds that gust
Rains that rust
Chilly nose
Woolen clothes
Birds don't sing—
I hate that autumn's far from spring.

Apple Picking

Shake the boughs,
Then throw the best
Into baskets.
(Leave the rest.)
Line them up
Upon a shelf.
Find a favorite:
Help yourself.
Purple skin
And yellow pulp.
Take a bite, then
 Gulp
      Gulp
           Gulp.

TREE-TICE

One leaf fell,
Then two,
Then three.
Such is autumn industree.
Four leaves fell,
Then five,
Then six.
A tree-tice on
Arithmetics.

Up and down

U^p ^{in a} ^{tree}
A screeching jay
Is teaching others:
Stay Away!
D
   o
     w
        n on the ground
A quiet squirrel
Buries acorns
For later referral.

AUTUMN QUESTIONS

How does a leaf f

            a

               l

                   l from a tree?
It happens autumnatically.
How does it find a new location?
Naturally, from autumn-ation.

Awe-tumn

When summer's seams
Have come undone,
Then greens to reds
And purples run.
A palette falls
To forest floor,
And autumn leaves
Leave me in awe.

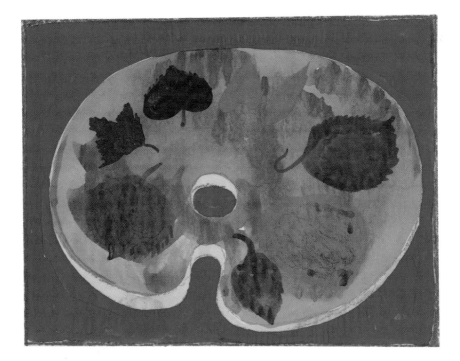

GEESE PIECE

Can

you

migration?

fall

tell

me

which

formation

do

geese

fly

in

Last licks

It's the last game of the year.
The last inning.
The last cheer.
The last batter.
The last swing.
And that has to *last*
Until the next spring.

OFF SEASON

Baseball is over.
The season is done.
But there's other ways
For a kid to have fun.
There's football and soccer,
Then hockey and skating,
Unless you like sitting
For six months, just waiting.

Indian summer

The calendar says it's almost November,
But poor Mother Nature forgot to remember:
November is frigid and freezing and chilly.
It's sixty degrees! Mother Nature looks silly.

HI-BEAR-NATION

Chipmunks, woodchucks
All sleep late.
Do brown bears really hi-bear-nate?
Moles and voles in burrows crawl.
Do brown bears slum-bear when it's fall?

THE WIND

Blow-drier.
Kite-flier.
Leaf-dancer.
Seed-prancer.
Hat-tosser.
Earth-crosser.

PLUMP PUMPKIN

Plump orange pumpkin.
Plump orange cat.
Plump orange full moon—
Orange you fat!

PUMPKINS GRIN

Once we were tiny.
Once we were green.
Now we are orange
To toast Halloween.
Soon we'll have noses,
Eyes and mouth too.
Then we will sneak up
Behind you and—
Boo!!!

Birds of autumn

Woodpecker,
Chickadee,
Crow,
And Owl.
Screech owls screech.
Horned owls scowl.
Starling,
Sparrow,
Cardinal,
Jay.
Guess the others
Flew away.

The owls

Barn owl.
Barred owl.
Spotted owl.
Screech.

Elf owl.
Horned owl.
BIG eyes each.

Long-eared.
Short-eared.
Owl.
Owlet.
All form nature's
Owlphabet.

A FALLING OUT

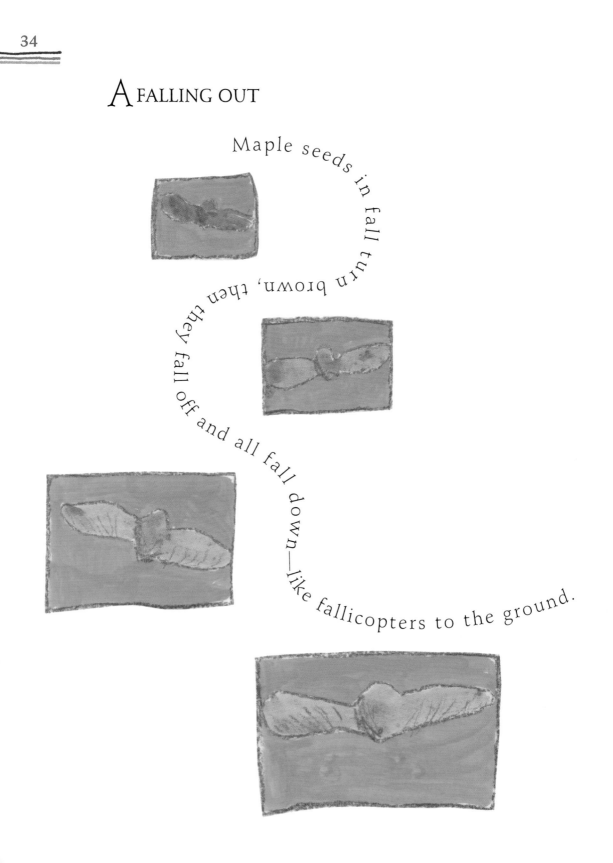

Maple seeds in fall turn brown, then they fall off and all fall down—like fallicopters to the ground.

THE COLORS OF AUTUMN

Burnt umber
Burnt sienna
Mars red
Orange henna
Silver gray
Olive green
Naples yellow
Tangerine
A touch of black
But not much blue—
Autumn's down-to-earth in hue.

Falling

An acorn falls
From an oak tree.
It falls through the air
And lands upon me.

A walnut falls
From a walnut tree.
It falls through the air
And lands upon me.

The temperature falls
Degree by degree.
It falls through the air
And lands upon me.

WHAT TO DO
WITH AUTUMN LEAVES

Kick them.
Catch them.
Pick them.
Snatch them.
Romp them.
Stomp them.
Hurl them.
Heave them.
If you want to,
Even *leave* them.

THANKSGIVING

Thanks for turkey.
Thanks for stuffin'.
Thanks for yams
And thanks for muffin.
Thanks for ease
And easy living.
Thanks for giving us
Thanksgiving.

AUTUMNESCENT

No crickets chirp.
No horseflies buzz.
No caterpillars
Full of fuzz.
The gnats are gone.
The June bug died.
The fall put each
Insect aside.

First frost

First frost,
First flake,
Fell on my nose
By mistake.

SYMMETREE

Autumn is the only season
The leaves all leave.
Call it tree-son.

Weathering

When autumn skies
Fill up with rain,
I soak it up.
I don't complain.

When autumn streets
With sleet get wet,
I splish and splash.
I do not fret.

When autumn hills
Fill up with snow,
Snow big deal.
I take it slow.

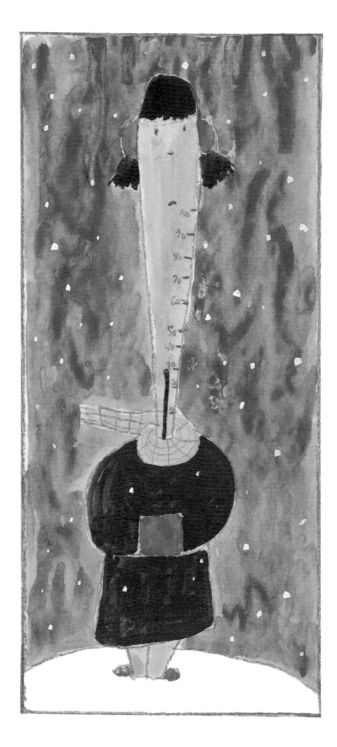

Brrrrrrr!

When leaves are brown
And red and gold,
That's when you feel
Octobrrrrr's cold.
When skies are crisp
And clear and still,
That's when you feel
Novembrrrrr's chill.
When autumn winds
Bend ends of trees,
That's when you feel
Decembrrrrr's freeze.

Naughtumn

The trees are bare.
The birds have flown.
What's going to grow
This year has grown.
The leaves fall down
And then get burned,
As autumn slowly gets winturned.